Cloud Animals

Having Fun With
Your Imagination

JASON STEIN

ISBN-13: 978-1507649503
ISBN-10: 1507649509

Dedication

To Griffin, Riley, and Trevor

Contents

Introduction

Imagination is more important than knowledge.
—Albert Einstein

One day I'm walking in the park and I see an oddly-shaped cloud in the sky. As I zoom in to take a picture of it, I notice it looks very much like a genie coming out of his genie lamp. After the cloud genie photo, I start collecting many cloud images and sort through them all to find around fifty that appear as cloud animals. As I get to know them better, they become their own characters, some with a sense of humor, and very friendly.

These are all real photographs I've taken, so let our journey with the cloud genie begin....

Cloud Animals

Genie and his Magic Lamp

Here is the genie cloud and he says to me, "this isn't your normal three wishes. As you go along your way remember to look up into the blue sky as you might find spectacular things of interest. So if you do see any cloud animals floating above, take the photo because you may never get another chance to capture them. And make sure to share what you have with others so that wherever people are in the world, they can also see the cloud animals floating high up in the sky."

With the help of my cloud genie, we go on a virtual carpet ride in the sky. Let's see what we find! Enjoy the ride!

Bat

Here's something unique: a bat that flies around during the day! Bats are nocturnal, but for the sake of this book, enjoy the rare chance to see a bat during the day.

Capybara

My genie lamp allowed me to see my first Capybara. Wow!

The Capybara is the world's largest rodent and is native to South America. They look like a cross between a guinea pig and a hippopotamus.

Capybaras love living in and near the water. They can weigh upwards of 100 pounds and can be found in many areas in zoos and parks. They are very vocal as well as social.

Capybaras are gentle and will usually allow humans to pet and hand-feed them.

Baby Chick

The sun was setting around this time, so what a nice surprise to see a pinkish-colored chick! Can't wait to see what it will look like all grown up.

Cali the Camel

Meet Cali the Camel. She is sitting on air and both her humps have eyes. She enjoys sightseeing and giving rides to her friends. She is wise, has great insight, and is always up for a good conversation! She is really, really good at staring contests.

Cloud Monsters Storm and Talon

Meet Storm and Talon. They love patrolling the sky together and when you hear rolling thunder, it just might be them, seeing who can roar the loudest. Either that or they laughed at one of their own jokes. Notice the small claws on the bottom of Storm's feet. Talon is above, telling Storm to do something about his cloud hair! It's one of those days. They are very interesting characters!

They also enjoy tummy rubs and the beginning of spring. I'm sure they would really like to meet you too!

Clyde the Crocodile

Watch out! This crocodile may mistake the lamp post for a juicy lamb post. Well, he's in for a light meal, don't you think?

Dinosaur

Rex the Dinosaur is running across the sky!
His favorite meal is a large T-bone steak!

An Elk and a Horse

To my surprise, there's a horse on the right side of the elk and it seems that one startled the other. Looks like Eva the Elk is curious enough to stick her neck out and find out what Harley the Horse is up to.

Roxy the Raven

See the tongue in her mouth. A raven with scary eyes!

Nickname: Devilish Bird
Favorite foods: Deviled eggs and popcorn

Phoenix

The Phoenix rises high in the sky once more!

The Phoenix is a mythical sacred bird that has a lifespan ranging from hundreds to thousands of years. For many cultures, the Phoenix represents high virtue, grace, peace, purity, power, prosperity, strength, and life.

Errol the Eagle

Eagles are amazing! I was lucky enough to get a glimpse of this one as it rose up from the clouds.

Eagles have very large hooked beaks, strong muscular legs, and powerful talons. Their beak is typically heavier than that of most other birds. Eagles' eyes are extremely powerful, enabling them to spot potential prey from a very long distance. Many countries also have an eagle as their national symbol.

Errol the eagle is excellent at helping you find your contact lenses if you drop them on the ground.

Cloud Rider on his Pony Express

The pony is running so fast his face is starting to break up! This is one of the most experienced cloud riders you'll find.

Buster the Big Bossy Dog

Really a sweetheart once you get to know him. He likes a nice barbeque party and stargazing!

Reginald the Labradoodle

Dog days of summer.
Does Reginald notice the bird flying below him?
He's just resting on his favorite spot, without a care in the world.

Cruising Dragon

This friendly flying dragon offered to give me flying lessons!

Totally unexpected! I was asked to cruise the wide open blue sky!

How cool is that?

Fire-Breathing Dragon

Now this is getting a little more entertaining!

How does a fire breathing dragon get so good at breathing fire?
Practice, practice, practice!

Dolly the Dragon

Dolly the Dragon can sniff out any goodies in the trees below. You can even make out her nostrils.

Elephant

Look at those ears. Inspired by Dumbo, Eli the Elephant really loves to fly!

He also enjoys long walks over water.

Francis the Frog

We call him Francis and you should see how he leaps from lily pad cloud to lily pad cloud.

Gorilla Family

Mamma gorilla with her babies (and maybe one nephew) in tow! All aboard!!!

Gus the Gorilla

Gus is always looking to make someone laugh. He performs regularly at the Sky Lounge.

Did you hear the one about…?
Can you be his audience?

Happy Dragon

Notice the scales on its back and the long tail as it flies through the sky.

What a great way to travel! Just hop on its back and go for a ride.

Buddy the Bridge Guardian

Notice the fine details outlining his mouth. It's nice to know Buddy the Bridge Guardian is watching over the bridge.

Hogarth the Hedgehog

There are some 15 species of hedgehog in Europe, Asia, and Africa.

Hedgehogs make pig-like grunts as they work through the hedges and that's how they got their name. Some people consider hedgehogs useful pets because they prey on many common garden pests. Hedgehogs have a coat of stiff, sharp spines, also known as quills. If attacked, they will curl into a ball that discourages most predators.

Safe to say, they don't make good seat cushions!

Hannah the Hippo

Did you know that the hippopotamus can easily outrun a person? Hippos have been clocked at 19 mph over short distances. The hippo is one of the most aggressive creatures in the world and ranks among the most dangerous animals in Africa.

Adult male hippos can weigh between 3,300 and 4,000 lbs. with older males reaching at least 7,100 lbs. The heaviest known hippo weighed almost 9,900 lbs. Now that's heavy!

Females are smaller than the males but some would say they are smarter!

Mamma and Baby Hippo

Where else can you see a mamma hippo playing with her baby hippo like this?

Only in the sky!

Show me a little hippo love! This is a once-in-a-lifetime experience!

Hippo Yawning

A hippo's lifespan is typically 40–50 years although the oldest recorded hippo lived until age 61.

Also, their teeth sharpen themselves as they grind together. The incisors can reach 1.3 ft, while the canines can reach up to 1.6 ft. The canines and incisors are used for fighting only, not in feeding. Hippos mainly eat grass and it seems they would need to eat a lot of it on a daily basis. Proceed with caution when around a hippo.

My hippo friends in the sky are all friendly and they have the biggest smile!

Lucy the Lamb

A lamb is a young sheep that is less than one year old. They always like to hang out in a flock (of sheep).

Wilma the Woolly Mammoth

The woolly mammoth was roughly the same size as our modern African elephants.

Males reached shoulder heights of between 9 and 11 ft and weighed up to 6.6 tons. Females averaged 8.5 to 9.5 ft in height. A newborn calf weighed about 200 lbs.

It's good to know we can still see them from time to time! They send their regards, and want you to look up once in a while and wave hello. You never know when one might be passing overhead. They are so big that sometimes when you hear thunder it just might be them walking by in the sky.

The Chase

They're at it again! They love playing tag. It's a very popular game among cloud animals. One cloud swallows up the other, then they start over. It looks like the little guy may get caught so let's cheer him on to get away so they can play again another day!

Mouse

Look, a mouse! A mouse is higher than a house!
Not only can there be a mouse under the house but now there is one
really big mouse over the house. And a very bright sun indeed.

Phoebe the Poodle

Also known as "Phoebe the bright one." She's really smart and likes to trick all the male poodles!

Plato the Pup

Say hi to Plato. He has a lot of energy and is very curious. There probably won't be a day that goes by where you won't see him playing around and chasing things.

Prancing Whoot

When I saw this, I knew it looked like something, but I couldn't put my finger on it. Why else would it appear out of the genie lamp? Here's this funny looking thing dancing or prancing around in the sky. We call him a Prancing Whoot!

Talk about seeing things from a different perspective. I took the Prancing Whoot cloud and changed the way I looked at it, and to my surprise, I found a most hidden beautiful creature that many don't get the chance to see.

Further along my journey see if you can tell what this is….

Praying Mantis

He is known as Monty and enjoys a cup of green tea while hanging out with his friends.

Proboscis Monkey/Kangaroo

This funny looking cloud animal is part proboscis monkey and part kangaroo. The endangered proboscis monkey has a prominent nose and lives only on the island of Borneo. The kangaroo part can travel far distances with a single sky hop!

Rabbit

This is the only rabbit that is closest to the stars! Speaking of stars, let's list some of the other rabbit stars we may know, shall we?

Bugs Bunny
Thumper
Roger Rabbit
Peter Rabbit
Harvey
Rabbit (*Winnie the Pooh*)
The White Rabbit (*Alice in Wonderland*)
The Rabbit of Caerbannog (*Monty Python and the Holy Grail*)

Seaburt the Seahorse

Some seahorse facts:

Seahorses are fish. They are bad swimmers and move very slowly, taking a long time to get anywhere. Seahorses are also experts at camouflage. They live around the world but are difficult to see in the wild. They are very still and blend in very well with their surroundings. See, this one looks like a cloud!

There are 54 species of seahorses and they range in size from under 1 inch to 14 inches long.

Sometimes Seaburt the Seahorse likes to visit the aquarium with his close friend, the Prancing Whoot. They both enjoy fine dining and bowling. And from a certain angle, they have been mistaken for twins. Hmmm!

Shark Head

Could it be? Maybe it's possible to have a sharknado after all! This is a friendly shark, who reminds me a little of the cartoon character Jabberjaw.

Sheldon the Sheepdog

There are 39 known breeds of sheepdog.

Sheepdogs guard sheep and other livestock on farms.

The Old English Sheepdog is stable and happy-go-lucky. It is able to adjust itself to different conditions, and is loving and friendly. It makes a fine family companion and is loyal, protective and intelligent. You can even tell that this sheepdog has bushy eyebrows over his eyes.

Sheldon likes funny bedtime stories and beautiful sunsets.

Sophie the Snake

Sophie the Snake is all coiled up under the sun.

Maybe she'll slither across your part of the sky, one of these days.

Sophie the Snake slithers through the sky singing silly songs about sunshine and sleet!

Try saying that three times fast!!

Socrates the Speedy Pup

On breezy afternoons, there is a good chance Socrates is out running around with Plato! Sometimes they play tag with Buster the Big Bossy Dog.

Sylvia the Stork

Storks can scoop anything out of the sky. They are long-necked wading birds with long, stout bills. They also make deliveries! Pizza, anyone?

Titus the Tortoise

Some "quick" facts about a tortoise:
Fact #1: There is nothing "quick" about a tortoise!

Tortoises are reptiles and like to live on land. They have mostly large dome-shaped shells which are heavier than those on turtles. Their feet are short and sturdy with bent legs. They eat fruits and veggies and their lifespan ranges from 80 to 150 years.

Wart Hog

This baby wart hog likes to play in the brush with her brothers and sisters.

When this appeared in the sky above me, I had no idea what it was, but I knew there was more than meets the eye. That little genie voice told me once again to take the shot and figure it out later. I had to shoot quickly because the wind was having its way that day!

Can you figure out what it looks like?
There are three images here, from what I can tell so far. Before you go to the next page, take a moment and see what you come up with. I reveal two of the three on the next photo.
OK, when you're ready, go to the next page....

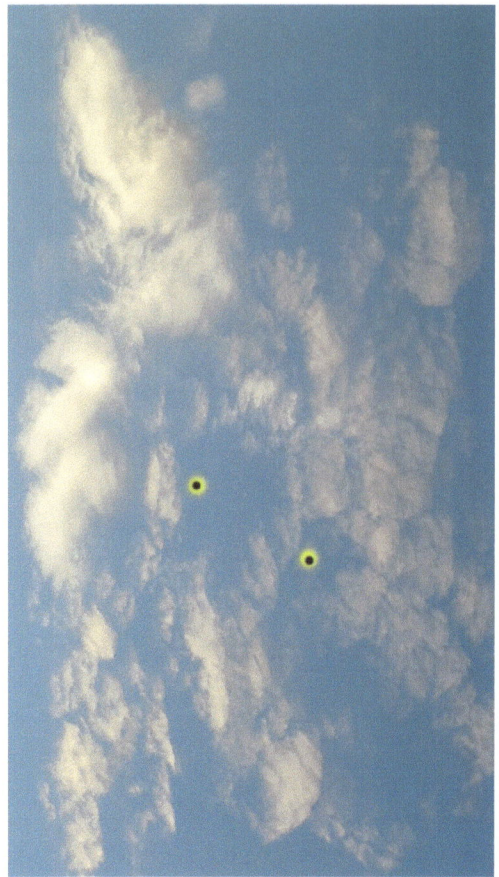

Big Bad Wolf

It looks like the Big Bad Wolf from Little Red Riding Hood.

Now on the left side of the wolf's face, below the left ear is one of the Easter Island Statues, which of course is much lighter than the real thing!

The third image was much trickier to see. I actually had to enlarge a section of the cloud image to get a better view. Do you see anything on the right side of the wolf? Take a moment to study it and the next page will reveal what this is.

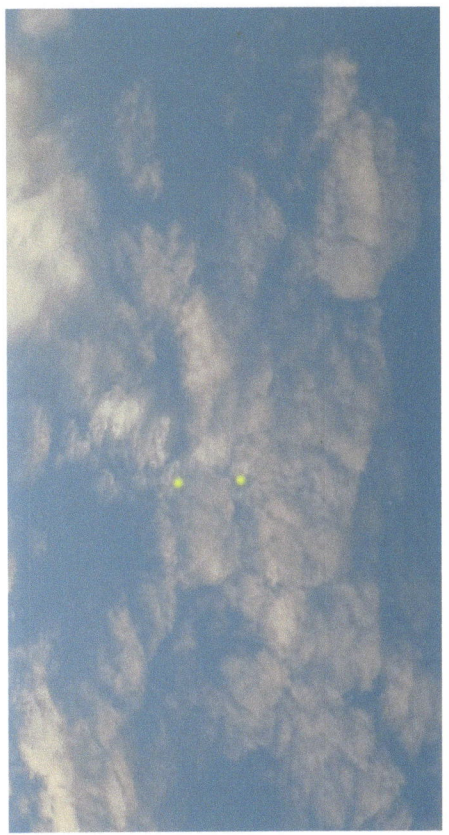

Old Man Winter

There is no slowing down for this guy! He's got that worn and rugged look. Oh, the winter of 2014 really kept him busy! Old Man Winter says it brought back memories of some other notable winters such as 1872-73, 1947-48, 1977-78 and 1995-96.

Celebrity Look-A-Like Clouds

Here are a couple of cloud images that resemble celebrities. You may recognize them!

ALF

ALF starred in his own show during the 1980s. He was very clever and always relied on his quick wit to get out of trouble.

Gonzo

(from The Muppets)

Gonzo always tries to do funny stunts that usually backfire.

Conclusion

Clouds are very unique and finding your own cloud genie is rare.

Taking this journey has revealed some very important (life) lessons:

One: Patience.

Two: When you see the cloud image, take the shot and don't procrastinate—it can be gone a second later.

Three: Creativity comes in many forms. We all have an imagination, regardless of our age. Don't be afraid to use it!

Four: Invest in a good pair of thin gloves when using a camera in cold weather! (I cannot stress this point enough.)

Five: Stay young at heart! You will enjoy life more!

Six: Cloud Genies are Awesome!

"Don't say you don't have enough time. You have exactly the same number of hours per day that were given to Helen Keller, Louis Pasteur, Michelangelo, Mother Teresa, Leonardo da Vinci, Thomas Jefferson and Albert Einstein." - H. Jackson Brown, Jr.

About the Author

Jason Stein has a background in stand-up comedy and improv. He is a licensed New York City tour guide and loves showing people around New York. He is also a certified practitioner of NLP(Neuro-Linguistic Programming) and is focused on showing people how to use humor as a coping mechanism and helping people find their passion. His website is www.thehappinesshelper.com. In his spare time, he indulges his fascination with clouds and enjoys walking through parks: they are wonderful places to allow one's imagination to run wild.

Disclaimer: No animals were injured during the making of this book.

www.ingramcontent.com/pod-product-compliance
Lightning Source LLC
Chambersburg PA
CBHW050821290526
45792CB00001B/214